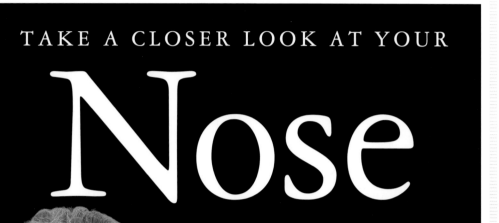

TAKE A CLOSER LOOK AT YOUR
Nose

BY JENNY FRETLAND VANVOORST

The Child's World®

Published by The Child's World®
1980 Lookout Drive • Mankato, MN 56003-1705
800-599-READ • www.childsworld.com

Acknowledgments
The Child's World®: Mary Berendes, Publishing Director
Red Line Editorial: Editorial direction and production
The Design Lab: Design
Content Consultant: Jeffrey W. Oseid, MD

Photographs ©: Jaimie Duplass/Shutterstock Images,
5, 23; Shutterstock Images, 6, 9, 10, 16, 18, 19, 24;
Arvind Balaraman/Shutterstock Images, 7; Inga Nielsen/
Shutterstock Images, 8; Alila Sao Mai/Shutterstock Images,
13; Brenda Carson/Shutterstock Images, 14; R.Classen/
Shutterstock Images, 15; Marco Mayer/Shutterstock Images,
21

Front cover: Arvind Balaraman/Shutterstock Images; Jaimie
Duplass/Shutterstock Images; Shutterstock Images

ISBN: 978-1623235468
LCCN: 2013931397

Printed in the United States of America
Mankato, MN
July, 2013
PA02175

About the Author

Jenny Fretland VanVoorst is a writer and editor of books for young people. She enjoys learning about all kinds of topics and has written books that range in subject from ancient peoples to artificial intelligence. When she is not reading and writing, Jenny enjoys kayaking, playing the piano, and watching wildlife. She lives in Minneapolis, Minnesota, with her husband, Brian, and their two pets.

Table of Contents

CHAPTER 1

Know Your Nose

How well do you know your nose? It is right in the middle of your face. You see it every day. But your nose does more than just hold up your glasses. It helps you breathe and smell. Your nose is made of bone, but it also has a small lump of **cartilage** at the tip.

Cartilage is flexible, so you can move your nose around. This flexible tip helps make your nostrils wide so you can take deeper breaths. Take a deep breath and fill your lungs with air. You may think the air is fresh and clean. But tiny **particles** of dust, dead skin, **pollen**, **bacteria**, and even insect parts float in the air.

Cartilage lets you wriggle and wrinkle your nose to make funny faces.

Your lungs need clean, warm air to work properly. Thank goodness you have a nose. Long or short, straight or upturned, your nose is in the perfect spot to catch the things floating in the air. On cold days, your nose warms the air you breathe in before it reaches your lungs.

The nose catches pollen before it reaches the lungs.

Particles can be bad for your lungs. But you would not be able to smell without them. That is because smells are actually tiny particles. These particles drift through the air, and your nose sniffs them up.

Small, solid scent particles are on objects all around us. What is your favorite scent?

Your nose has scent **receptors** to help you catch the smell particles in the air. Sometimes your nose picks up scent particles that are not so fun! Did you know your nose could help save you from a fire? The scent receptors help you smell the smoke. Then your nose helps filter out the smoke to keep the air in your lungs clean.

Every person can recognize as many as 10,000 different smells!

Scent receptors in your nose can act like a smoke detector to let you know there is a fire.

You can plug your nose to keep smelly scent particles out.

CHAPTER 2

The Nose Job

Your nose has many different jobs. It is part of the **respiratory system**. This is the body system that helps you breathe. Your lungs are also part of the respiratory system. But lungs are hidden deep inside your chest.

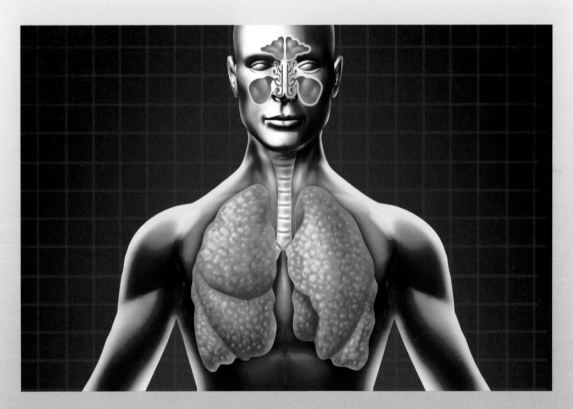

Your nose and lungs work together to help you breathe.

When you breathe in with your nose, air enters into your nostrils. Lungs pull the air in. Then the air goes through little hallways called **nasal passages**. In the nasal passages, short stubbly hairs filter the air. These hairs catch particles that could damage your lungs. An area called the **nasal cavity** is at the top of the nasal passages. This is where the nose picks up smells.

Your nose and mouth are the only parts of the respiratory system you can see.

Some particles make it past the hairs in the nasal passages. They get swept up and mixed with **mucus**. Your nose makes more than one quart (1 liter) of mucus a day. So what happens to all that mucus? It just slips down the back of your throat. You swallow it along with your food without noticing.

Scent particles are like puzzle pieces. Each one has a special spot it fits in. When a piece fits, special nerves send a signal to the brain. The brain compares that scent with scents you have already smelled. Is it a flower? Or is it a new smell?

Nasal Passages

Nasal Cavity

Cartilage

Nostril

Left Lung

Right Lung

Your nose can also help you remember. Have you ever smelled something that made you feel good? That is because the brain thinks about the scents you smell in the same part of the brain that controls your emotions and memory.

Did you know your dog can smell better than you? A dog's sense of smell can be 100,000 times better than a human's.

Maybe the smell of freshly baked cookies brings back a good memory.

Humans have about 5 million scent receptors, but dogs have more than 220 million!

CHAPTER 3

When the Nose Knows Trouble

Your nose is a hard worker. If you get sick, your nose has an even bigger job to do. Your nose makes extra mucus when you have a cold. This mucus clogs up your nasal passages. It also blocks scent particles. That is why it can be hard to smell when you have a cold.

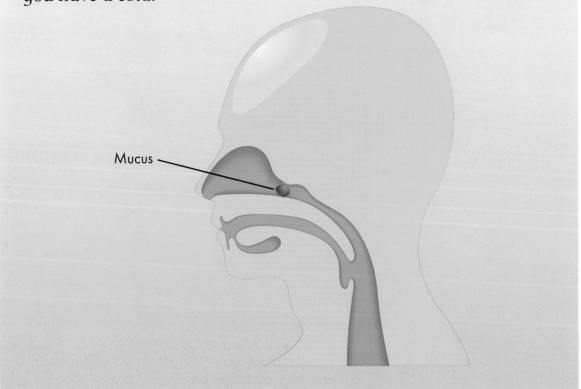

Mucus

Nosebleeds happen when **blood vessels** inside the nose break. Having a bunch of blood rush out of your nose can be scary. But nosebleeds look worse than they really are. If you get a nosebleed, lean forward so the blood does not go down your throat. Use a tissue to catch the blood. Then pinch the tip of your nose to slow down the flow.

Your ears, nose, and throat are all connected by a tube. That is why your throat and your nose can both hurt when you have a cold.

Some nose problems happen as you get older. As you age, you start to lose your sense of smell. You may think your grandmother's house smells a bit musty. But she probably can't tell!

CHAPTER 4
Protect Your Nose

Your nose does not need a lot of special care. But be gentle on it. It is better to blow your nose than to pick it. Picking it can move germs from your fingers into your nose. It can also break blood vessels and cause a bloody nose.

Use a tissue when blowing your nose to avoid spreading germs.

If you are around dust, wear a mask over your nose and mouth. The mask will block bigger particles so they cannot reach your nose.

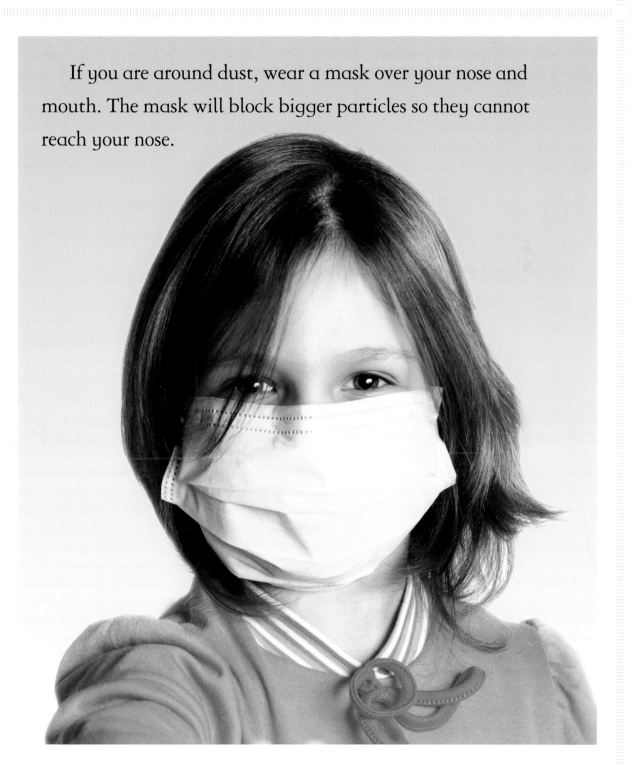

A mask can protect your nose and lungs from particles and germs.

When you breathe in dry air, your mucus can dry out. It crusts up and sticks to the inside of your nose. This is sometimes called a booger.

Dry air can make your nose more sensitive. If your nose is dry and irritated, moister air may help your nose feel better. Ask your parent or guardian if a humidifier makes sense for your home.

Your nose is very busy. It helps you breathe and smell. And sometimes it even helps you remember. Who knew that object in the middle of your face could do so much? Take good care of your nose. Get to know your nose so you can help take care of this amazing organ.

Take care of your nose so you can continue to smell your favorite foods.

GLOSSARY

bacteria (bak-TEER-ee-uh) Bacteria are very tiny living things that exist all around you and in you. Some bacteria are useful, but some cause disease.

blood vessels (bluhd VES-uhlz) Blood vessels are small tubes inside the body that blood flows through. Tiny blood vessels in the nose can break and cause a nosebleed.

cartilage (KAHR-tuh-lij) Cartilage is a strong, elastic tissue that connects bones in humans and other mammals. The tip of the nose is made of cartilage.

mucus (MYOO-kuhs) Mucus is a slimy fluid you sometimes blow out of your nose. Mucus coats and protects the inside of your mouth, nose, and throat.

nasal cavity (nay-zuhl KAV-i-tee) The nasal cavity is the empty space at the top of the nose. The nose picks up smells in the nasal cavity.

nasal passages (NAY-zuhl pas-ij-uhz) Nasal passages are the pathways air takes on its way to the lungs. Little hairs in the nasal passages filter out particles.

particles (PAHR-ti-kuhlz) Particles are extremely small pieces of something. The nose helps filter out small particles before they reach the lungs.

pollen (PAH-luhn) Pollen is made of tiny yellow grains from flowers. Pollen can cause allergic reactions in some people.

receptors (ri-SEPT-orz) The parts of your body that receive information and turn it into a signal are called receptors. Scent receptors in your nose help you catch and identify smells.

respiratory system (RES-pur-uh-tor-ee sis-tuhm) The respiratory system is the body system that helps you breathe. The nose and mouth are the only visible parts of the respiratory system.

LEARN MORE

BOOKS

Douglas, Lloyd G. *My Nose.* New York: Children's Press, 2004.

Parker, Steve. *The Senses.* Chicago: Raintree, 2004.

Stewart, Melissa. *Up Your Nose!* New York: Marshall Cavendish Benchmark, 2010.

WEB SITES

Visit our Web site for links about the nose: **childsworld.com/links**

Note to Parents, Teachers, and Librarians: We routinely verify our Web links to make sure they are safe and active sites. So encourage your readers to check them out!

INDEX